The God Of The Mundane

The God
Of The Mundane

Reflections on Ordinary Life
for Ordinary People

by Matthew B. Redmond

The God of the Mundane

Published by:

Kalos Press, an imprint of Doulos Resources; PHONE: (901) 201-4612; WEBSITE: www.doulosresources.org.

Please address all questions about rights and reproduction to Doulos Resources; PHONE: (901) 201-4612; E-MAIL: info@doulosresources.org.

Published 2012

Printed in the United States of America by Ingram, Inc.

ISBNs:

978-1-937063-96-2 (trade paperback edition)
978-1-937063-95-5 (electronic/digital editions)

Library of Congress Catalogue Number: 2012954084

Cover design by J.E. Eubanks, Jr.

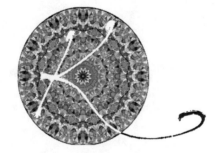

For Bethany

We work our fingers down to dust

And we wait for Kingdom Come

With the radio on

~ Gaslight Anthem

Contents

Introduction

"I'm 40, I have a Master's degree, and now I'm having to learn how to be a bank teller."

Me

When I wrote *The God of the Mundane*, it was the work of a pastor. I felt like I had seen something encouraging — liberating — for those who were in my charge and beyond. And I heard as much from those who had read the initial blog posts.

The goal was to comfort Christians where they were — to help people believe the mundane stuff matters.

And I had two people in mind as I wrote. Others moved in and out of my mind and were a huge help, but these two held my hand the whole way. They were ideals, working like muses.

The first is a stay-at-home mom. She does the same chores everyday. She fixes meals not always appreciated. She changes diapers, does laundry, dusts, does homework, sweeps and heals sick kids, world without end. And then she goes to church and hears sermons, or is recommended books that make her sick with worry that she is not doing enough. She is no one in particular, and every stay-at-home mom I know. I didn't choose her to be in the forefront of my mind because she is to be idolized. It would be more truthful to say this picture of a mom chose me.

So, she was with me the whole way.

But there was another. A man, stuck. Stuck in a job that feels small — a job making him feel small. He is not embarrassed of his job so much as just miserable. On Monday, he can

1

barely stay awake because he's been awake since 3:45 dreading the day ahead. Sometimes he is so full of anger at his plight.

He believes the gospel but has no idea what that means for him in this dead-end job. He also reads books and hears sermons. And they make his work feel even smaller.

Actually, if we want to be specific about it, he is a banker. When I wrote this book, I didn't know what bankers did, so all I could picture is a guy working in the drive-thru trying to balance his drawer. It sounded miserable to me. It was a picture of unimaginable frustration.

And I wanted this guy to believe in the God of the mundane. I wanted this guy to see that this is the work of those who have the Spirit in full. I was desperate to make him see it is not only the work of missionaries and ministers that matters. I wanted him to believe his work is inherently spiritual and good. Even if he hates it each and every moment.

But I'm not a pastor anymore. And this morning, my boss made it clear I would be training to do something that drives fear right through me like arrows. Though hired to ride a desk, I will be trained to be a bank teller when needed.

This is but the latest wave in a never-ending rhythmic tide of disappointment. And it feels like the belly of a whale sometimes.

At other times I can barely hold it together. I'm forty years old and often want to cry like a schoolgirl because I am miserable with my job. And I'm not very good at it.

Did you know you have to be able to count to be a banker?

You laugh, but I was the last one to learn long division in fourth grade and I still have not caught up.

Is it Providence that makes me need the very thing I labored for others to see? Whatever you call it, I'm having to hang onto my own words. If I over-analyze myself here, it feels like arrogance. But it's really very humbling, swallowing the medicine you wanted to convince everyone was good for them.

It don't go down so easy.

Listen, I wrote the book but that is no indication of this being easy for me to accept. There are so many days I feel abandoned and cast off. It's hard most days for me to think of my work as inherently good, and as significant in the Kingdom as the work I did as a pastor.

But even though I secretly harbor a deep enjoyment of

painting my job as filled with horror daily, there are moments of radiant light.

For every customer who tells me I am not good at what I do and I should go back to doing what I did before — that really happened — there is an Alyssa.

Alyssa, 20 years old, came in one afternoon, not long before closing. She had a negative balance and looked like her world was ending. Because it was. She had a check to deposit, but much of the funds were going to be eaten up by the negative balance.

She whispered, "I suck at life."

In an effort to stall while trying to think of a solution she reluctantly told me she needed to be able to pay the co-pay before her cancer treatment. Earlier in the year she had been given the diagnosis.

Before she was done telling me the details, we were both in tears. I ceased being a banker and instead I was talking with a young person again like I did so often as a pastor. Stalling worked: I came up with a solution and she left with promises of prayer and her money.

I called to check back in on her after she told me she would be done. She was not able to talk yet but called me back the next day. She sounded even sadder. They had found tumors now in her lymph nodes and chest.

Silence. The kind of silence that has the weight of the world fixed squarely upon its shoulders.

She then told me how she would have to quit her job. She had already given up a cheerleading scholarship...the way she told me this, it had the tone of a death-knell. She knew she was basically getting terrible news. I promised to pray for her and check in again soon.

Three days later she came in with another paycheck. She made a beeline to my office. "I don't need anything today, I could've gone thru the drive-thru but I wanted to tell you that the tumors are benign!"

And so we both teared up again. That was just over a week ago. I'm having more good days at work now since.

I've stared down into the faux-wood grain of my desk and cursed the moment I ever sat down behind it. I've had so many days where I was on the verge of emotionally losing control, I had to leave my desk and go look at myself in the mirror and let my gray hairs remind me I am a grown man. My tie was a noose and my nametag felt like a guilty verdict.

But since that day, I've seen my desk as now a place where holy things can happen. It's often felt like an altar — a place of sacrifice — but working with Alyssa confirmed it. My tie felt like a clerical collar. My name tag, a sign of favor.

The more I've thought about Alyssa and her story, the more I've realized how much I would not have wanted to be anywhere else.

Look, I've pretty much lived on Monster.com and other sites over the past six months. I've talked to people about other jobs. I've interviewed and the only reason I'm still where I am is that no one really wants a pastor who smells like he's been in the belly of a whale. Or I'm not qualified.

Whichever.

But it all feels like Providence now. Banks are supposed to be cold halls of greed and indifference. And I can see why: it's all about numbers. But I was able to cut across the expectations with words.

And as I've looked back, there have been more stories like Alyssa's. There is the mother whose son was stealing from her account to buy drugs between stints in prison. So I'm still counseling parents about their kids.

And I was able to instill some hope into some newlyweds who had too much dreadful expectation heaped on them since exchanging vows. No one had told them the good news of marriage till I did.

I've sat in front of a man whose wife had just asked for a divorce the day before.

Once I asked a mom and son why they had come into the branch today only to find out Dad/ex-husband had just killed himself the day before.

I didn't handle all these situations perfectly. And sometimes I may have failed to represent Christ as some might want me to. So, I'm not bragging on myself.

I'm bragging on the mundane and the God thereof.

I'm 40, I have a Master's degree, and now I'm having to learn how to be a bank teller. In other words, I've found myself right smack dab in the middle of the very experience I wanted to speak into. And after almost a year of having to drink deeply of the draught I once only prescribed, I believe more than ever there is a God of the mundane.

CHAPTER ONE

The Question of the Mundane

"We often let the big ideas, the majestic vistas of salvation, the grand visions of God's work in the world, and the great opportunities for making an impact in the name of Jesus distract us from taking with gospel seriousness the unglamorous ordinary."

Eugene Peterson,
*Practice Resurrection: A Conversation
on Growing Up in Christ*

"My life is so damn mundane."

One of 10,000 voices on Twitter

A young mother spends yet another morning scraping last night's mac and cheese off the linoleum. A barista rises at 4 a.m. and slogs into work so everyone else can get coffee on their way. Behind a uniform desk, a well-starched banker sits and analyzes numbers. Underneath a luxury SUV, a mechanic reaches for greasy tools while Springsteen plays in the background. A room full of 3rd graders challenges the wit, patience, and energy of a young teacher. A father has a lightsaber battle with his son. Comfortably dressed, a librarian rises and points to the section where books on how to pass the GED are correctly shelved. Outside of an empty house, a real estate agent is waiting for an eager family. A nurse delivers medicine to sometimes-thankful patients. A graphic designer stares at a screen dreaming for the sake of others. A mother gets up to change another diaper.

And I wonder:

Is there a God of the mundane?

As I look around the landscape of evangelicalism, the world I find myself in, the mundane escapes notice. The ordinary is given lip-service, but overlooked like the garnish on a steak dinner. What the evangelical church really wants is something as large as God Himself, whether personality or performance, workers or windfalls.

The call is to do something big. I've sat on the edge of my front-row seat and heard the call thundered from pulpits. And I've been the one thundering:

> *"Change the world," I can hear myself crying out. "Change your world. Change the world of someone. Anyone. Sell everything. Sell anything. Give it away. Do something crazy. Be radical. Make people stand up and notice. Take a risk. Jesus moved from heaven to earth and gave up his life and yet you — you just go about your daily life."*

All too easily I can hear myself burdening the room with words, phrases, and ideas I've heard elsewhere:

> *"Your days should be blood-earnestly marked by an urgent, nerve-twisting love for people you have never known," I might say. "And if you truly loved them you would join the missions team's trip at the expense of your vacation to know them. If you loved God, you would do it. And if you really believed-BELIEVED, you would go and stay. You should want to go. It should be hard to stay where you are in the comfort of where you are."*

My own voice, like a lance, slashes through the darkness in every soul before me:

> *"You worship," I berate them. "And then what do you do? You rest. You huddle in your house with your spouse and kids. You eat. You drink. You make love. Go to your kid's games. Go out with friends. You have clean sheets, clean stainless-steel refrigerators and clean water. You change nothing while millions die in poverty. Each week is a brick used to build the house of a wasted ordinary existence."*

I've heard all of it flail in my own head and lash against my ribs, leaving sourness in my stomach no medicine can aid. Worse: similar words, if not these very ones, I turned into whips with which to waken the consciences of those sitting before me. It never felt right but it preached well.

No lie. I used to preach and teach like this. And if I didn't use the exact words and draw the precise conclusions, I let the listener fill them in like some twisted religious Mad-Lib.

But then I began to ask questions. The inconvenient ones.

Really? Is this the normal Christian life? Is God sitting around waiting for each and every believer to do something monumental? Is this the warp and woof of the New Testament? Are the lifestyles of the Apostles the standard for the persons in the pew? Are the first-century believers the standard?

Is this our God?

In the economy of God, do only the times when we are doing something life-changing have any spiritual cache with Him?

Does He look over the mundane work of the housewife only to see the missions trip she may go on?

So, I wondered. I wondered about the great majority I have known and know. The great majority living fairly ordinary lives.

Is there a God, for instance, for those who are not changing anything but diapers? Is there a God for those who simply love their spouse and pour out rarely-appreciated affection on their children day after day? Is there a God for the mom who spends what feels like God-forsaken days changing diapers and slicing up hot dogs? Is there a God for the men who hammer out a day's work in obscurity for the love of his wife and kids? Is there a God for just and kind employers? Generous homemakers? Day-laborers who would look at a missions trip to Romania like it was an unimaginable vacation?

Is there a God for the middle-class mom staving off cancer, struggling to raise teenagers and simply hoping both Mom and Dad keep their job? Is there a God for the broken home with a full bank account but an empty bed? Is there a God for grown children tending to the health of their aged parents?

Is there a God, who delights in the ordinary existence of the unknown faithful doing unknown work? Is there a God of grace for those who live out their faith everywhere but do not want to move anywhere?

Is there a God for those who have bigger homes than me? More money than me? Nicer cars than me? Better health than me?

Is there a God for the mundane parts of life, the small moments? Is there a God of kind smiles, good tips and good mornings? Is there a God of goodbye hugs and parting kisses? What about firm, truthful handshakes and grasps of frail fingers in sanitized hospital rooms?

Does God care about the forgotten mundane moments between the sensational, those never remembered? Or are those spiritually vacuous moments for which there is no God?

Is there a God of the mundane?

Does this God I worship care about mundane people and moments?

I'm not crazy. I know there are others asking the same question. But it felt like the lonely question we ask into the night sky where no one will answer. And when we can finally ask it, the comfort is not in the answer so much as wishing we could hear others asking the same question. If misery loves company, a company of wondering would have been nice.

But I kept looking into that night sky. It began looking less empty with all its stars and planets and blank blackness. And the question, hanging there, caught in the beauty of the firmament, yearned for an answer echoing throughout the constellatory.

Perhaps I should give full disclosure. None of these thoughts are of the disinterested sort. I need to answer the question for myself. I've already answered the question before it: can I while away my days in obscurity? And so answering in the affirmative and consigning myself to a mundane existence, I now ask: is there now a God of grace for me and my work — in the days that turn into weeks, into months and years, never distinguished but in the need for a new calendar?

Should I want something bigger? Will God be for me then?

Is God for my wife, whose days are full of conversations with children, repeated trips to the store, dirty diapers, floors that have to be swept and clothes to be washed constantly? Is there a God for her when one of our three children is sick, confused and full of tears pouring out of wide-eyed sockets and mixing with her own? Is there a God for her as she slowly moves away from youth and into a frame she can hardly believe is her own?

Should she want more? Will He only be her God if she does something "big?"

As I write this, I'm a pastor. And the question looms large. It hangs in the air where I study and over the pulpit. The question stretches out into the pew where it steals away into suburban homes and places of work and various schools. It breaks into bedrooms and boardrooms.

Is there a God for the mundane parts of our lives? For our mundane lives? Is there a God who makes sense of the life lived between the seismic and extraordinary? Between the missions trips? In between the joy and the pain? Is there a God for the meantime in a culture drunk on the weekend's promises?

I think there is.

CHAPTER TWO

The Answer of the Mundane

The most extraordinary thing in the world is an ordinary man and an ordinary woman and their ordinary children.

G.K. Chesterton

My goal is not to call anyone "mundane." I just assume you've done it yourself.

I write all this under the assumption that everyone at some point stops what they are doing, frustrated. They put their face in the palms of tired hands. Or they look up. And they ask, "does this matter?"

Does my work and life and all its parts matter at all? To God? To anyone?

It happens after reading a magazine article about a celebrity. It happens after years of doing the same thing day after day after day. And it could be happening right now because you just got back from lunch with a friend whose life is exciting, comparatively speaking.

Or it happens after a sermon.

My hope is for you to read, on every page of this little book, that there is a God of the mundane.

Yes: there is a God for those who are not changing anything but diapers. There is a God for those who simply love their spouse and pour out unappreciated affection on their children, day after day. There is a God for the mom who spends her days scraping the trampled mac and cheese off the kitchen floor. There is a God for the man who hammers out a day's work in obscurity for his wife and kids. There is a God for the just and kind employers. There is a God for generous home-makers, generous with prayers and dollars and time. There is a God for day-laborers looking at a missions trip to the far corners of the world like an unimaginable vacation.

There is a God for the middle-class people staving off can-cer, struggling to raise teenagers, and simply hoping against hope they keep their jobs. There is a God for the broken home with a full bank account but an empty bed. There is a God for those children tending to the health of their aged parents.

There is a God delighting in the ordinary existence of the unknown faithful doing unknown work. There is a God of grace for those who live out their faith everywhere but do not want to move anywhere.

And there is even a God for those who have bigger homes, more money, nicer cars and better health than me.

And yes, there is a God of the mundane parts of life, the small moments. There is a God of kind smiles, good tips, and good mornings. There is a God of goodbye hugs and parting kisses. A God of firm handshakes. A God of grasping, frail fingers in hospital rooms.

There is a God of all the forgettable moments between the sensational, never remembered. These are not spiritually vacu-ous moments for which there is no God.

There is a God for those pastors who while away in mun-dane work: for those whose days turn into weeks, months, years, only distinguished by the need for a new calendar. There is a God for the mundane moments of ministry.

There is a God for those like my wife, whose days are full of trying conversations with children, repeated trips to the store for clean diapers, floors that have to be swept and clothes needing to be washed, world without end. There is a God when our children are sick, confused and full of tears over a lost sock. There is a God for wives, for women as they move away from youth and into a frame they can hardly believe is their own.

There is a God for those with mundane lives. There is a God who can make sense of the life lived between the seis-mic and the extraordinary, between the joy and the pain. Yes. There is a God for the mean times in a culture drunk on the weekend's promises.

This is an encouraging answer.

Encouraging because most of us live very mundane lives. Encouraging because so much of our life is full of the mundane.

We wake up in the morning. Shower. Dress in last year's fashions. Eat the same breakfast we did the day before. Kiss our significant other. Kiss the kids. Go to work or stay home for the work that never ends. We have supper. Watch some TV. Do it again.

Though we enjoy vacations and short seasons of excitement, we for the most part have ordinary days. And expect to for the rest of them.

We will not be famous. We will not be stars in our culture's glittering nights. And though many of us have drunk deeply of a celebrity-saturated world, we live a life apart. Oh, we want to be famous, known and revered. But that is not the reality. The reality is no one will write books about us. And outside of our families, we will be forgotten.

This sounds terrible but only because fame — which was never ours — has obscured our view of what really is. And what is that? That we are part of that not so exclusive group of men and women throughout history known as "everyone else."

Christians are not immune to the problem of being mundane and seeing it as a problem. We have breathed in the same fumes as the rest. Our hearts burn for our deeds to be noticed and celebrated. We want to do something big and have it thrust into cyberspace for all to read. Those who follow the Man of no reputation pine for one,[1] résumés ready.

There are dark and dusty corners of our heart that will fight tooth-and-nail against ever being known to exist.

---

1 Phillipians 2:6-7 (ESV): *who, though he was in the form of God, did not count equality with God a thing to be grasped, but emptied himself, by taking the form of a servant, being born in the likeness of men.* King James Version uses the words *made himself of no reputation.*

The reason is easy to see. We think the small, mundane, ordinary things we do each and every day are worth nothing before God because they are worth nothing before the gods of this world.

But even the famous cannot escape. And they will try just like us. They will leverage all their money and talent and influence to burst the bonds of the mundane. But they are also bound, and bound tight, as we are.

We may envy their lifestyle. But if we were to look closely we would see much that could only be called mundane. And while we are trying to escape the mundane, many of the famous desire more of it.

It is encouraging that there is a God of the mundane, because lives are just that — mundane. This is good news for those who have tired of trying to live fantastically. And this is spectacular news for those who have been tempted to think their lives escape the notice of God because they are decidedly not spectacular.

It is encouraging because the mundane is reality. We may flirt with greatness, but the fact is — for the Christian and non-Christian — ordinary is the divine order of the day for the vast majority of us. Kids, bills, coupons, cable, home repair, gas in the tank, church attendance, inexpensive pleasures, discount shopping and family reunions are what we are made of.

Sure, there are explosive interruptions — wondrous and terrible — which are inevitable. Indeed, how many of the stories we love are tales of the ordinary man or woman whose life is changed by extraordinary events and nothing is the same again. Prince Charming rides in. A goddess steps out of the wood. All is terrifically unhinged.

But for the most part, all is mundane. Ordinary. Thankfully, there is a God behind it all.

CHAPTER THREE

The Apostle Paul or
the Person in the Pew?

Sometimes I envy those who are reading the Bible for the first time. It's all unfamiliar virgin territory, fresh and new. The world is under their feet but it moves as they read, and the heavens open in terrible glory. They get lost in the meaning of the stories, and teachings, and songs, and poems, and prophecies. And they know they are lost. (The way I feel when reading James Joyce.) Knowing we are lost is helpful. Humility comes like a friend and we then allow ourselves to ask for help.

I've been reading all these bizarre and beautiful stories and teachings and songs and poems and prophecies my whole life long. They mark my life as scars do on proud old veterans. They are so familiar that I cannot escape many of them. Without any help they rush to the scene to help me make sense of everything. And while familiarity has not led to contempt, it has led to other problems.

I hardly ever feel lost.

I hardly ever get to be helpless when I read the Bible. Almost forty years of hearing it, a Biblical Studies degree and a Master of Divinity will conspire to make one proud. It is good that the Bible has been my lifelong companion. It is not good to think I'm never lost in my reading it.

This lesson was taught to me in a particularly painful way about a year before I wrote this.

For as long as I can remember I had been reading the letters to the churches in the New Testament and missing something. I missed it as a young man wanting to enter vocational ministry, and I missed it as a seminary student. I sadly missed it as a pastor. Sometimes we may miss things because they are hidden. But we seem to always miss much because we see it every day.

I missed the obvious: the Apostles are writing to normal people.

Most of them are nameless. They are Jew and Gentile, yes. But they are also *not* apostles. And most are not pastors. They are carpenters, farmers, traders, sailors, fisherman, shepherds, guards. They are mothers and fathers and children. Compared to the life of an apostle, their lives are probably mundane. These are ordinary men and women believing an extraordinary story.

They are not the Apostle Paul, or Peter, or any of the other apostles, who are immortalized in the pages of sacred writ. They are ordinary people who huddled in someone's home, drank their wine, ate their bread, and listened to the Holy Spirit through the words of an Apostle. And then they went home. And they got up the next morning and lived a normal life, probably to the end of their days.

And now, poof! They are forgotten.

My guess? Most of them lived out the rest of their lives after coming to faith with the most exciting thing in their lives being when they believed and aligned themselves with Christ and his people. They kept on living where they were and making a living as they did before they believed. They lived normal lives. Only more so.

They listened to Paul's teaching, learned from him, and in faith stayed where they were after he left.

All of this should have been obvious to me but it wasn't. For years I read and thought and then taught as if Paul was the standard for those I was teaching. "Look at Paul and his singular devotion to Christ," I would implore them. And then it hit me. The nameless, ordinary believer who listened to Paul and lived faithfully as a farmer, mother, etc., right where they were — they are the standard. The forgotten mundane existence of those whose names we will never know is the endgame.

It is true Paul says to his readers, "imitate me..."[1] And he says it more than once. In each instance, Paul wants his readers to see that he is an example of what he is asking of them in

---

1 I Corinthians 11:1; 4:16; 2 Thessalonians 3:9 (ESV)

that particular context. His life is consistent with what he is teaching. He isn't out of step.

But he never asks them to stop being who they are. He never challenges them to go anywhere. We don't even get hints that lead us to believe he is making them feel guilty for living in comparative comfort compared to his lack of it. That's weird. And it's weird because this is so common in our pulpits and in conferences held for zealous college students.

It is not enough to be among the ordinary. The spirituality of the unknown recipients of Paul's letters is not enough for us. It is not enough to be a believing mother of small children; we feel as if we should have the spirituality of doing it overseas. With bullets flying overhead. And malaria crouching outside.

Someone recently asked me which missionary biographies they should read. I am not sure why she asked. But I've been asked before. And I did know she was studying to be something other than a missionary.

So I told her to read a biography of a Christian banker first. By that I meant she needed to read a book about a Christian living a mundane life. She told me she could not find one. Figures.

For some this whole idea of identifying with the person in the pew instead of the Apostle Paul will be a challenge. Maybe it will feel like a death, death to a dream of being someone special, out of the ordinary and above the fray. The idea of being one of the forgotten is formidable.

But for countless others this is the second greatest piece of news they have ever heard. "Wait, it's all right for me to be ordinary? I can live a mundane existence and not feel guilty about it? You mean, the call on my life is for me to be faithful right where I am?"

So many pastors today, famous ones and otherwise, are asking young people and everyone else if they are willing to give it all and go overseas as a missionary. It's not a bad question to ask. There is no question in my mind that this question needs to be out there. But they — or someone — also needs to ask, "are you willing to be numbered among the nameless believers in history who lived in obscurity? Do you have the courage to be forgotten by everyone but God and the heavenly host? Are you willing to be found only by God as faithful right where you are? Are you willing to have no one write a book about you and what you did in the name of Christ? Are you willing to live and believe — in stark contrast to the world around you — there is a God of the mundane?"

CHAPTER FOUR

"It Helps"

J ust before I get out of my car to walk into the library where I write, my phone alerts me to a dentist appointment. This is my one-hour warning. Crap.

What do I do now?

So I drive back up the mountain that I live on, from which I had just minutes before descended. I find a parking lot. I should try to write but I am so frustrated I pull out a Mary Karr book to read and dull the pain. Plus, writing in a car is hard.

So for 40 minutes, I read.

With a few minutes to spare I step out of Karr's hard-luck life and into the waiting room. After signing in, I sit down in front of months-old editions of *Motor Trend* and *Sports Illustrated*. Billy Joel plays in the background. It was just me and the receptionist.

Anger wells up inside. *Writing*, I need to be writing. Not lying in a sterile chair with a hygienist's hands in my mouth, listening to soft rock while staring at the ceiling where the flavors of toothpaste are listed, color-coded.

Like a bad dream, Celine Dion comes on and I get really mad.

Eventually Candace, my hygienist, comes to get me.

"Are you ready?"

I wonder which would be worse: to sit here with Celine Dion or go back to the dentist chair.

We walk back through the maze of offices and rooms of other patients, and I keep turning in the wrong direction. Celine follows me regardless. A lose-lose.

I step in, sit down, and hear the plastic of the chair squeal as my backside slides into place. In front of me is one of those digital picture frames flashing kids and memories. Candace's daughter is on the sequined color guard team at the University of Alabama. So, I have to look at the enemy school's colors in every single picture.

There are other little knick knacks and pictures sitting around the room.

So now I'll come to youuuuuuu with oooooopen arms...

Candace pushes a button. The chair hums like it will take off through the ceiling. I look up and see the word "raspberry." X-rays are needed. The film is put in my mouth and the pictures are taken.

Candace never stops smiling. Her conversation puts me at complete ease. OK, maybe not complete ease. But I do feel safe here, as safe and easy as one can feel in a dentist's chair. There is the distinct air of hospitality there in that room. And the smell of whatever they keep everything so clean with.

This hospitality is preferable to the silent treatment of some dental hygienists. If someone is going to stick their fingers in my mouth and inflict pain on me in the process, I would prefer a kind smile and amiable one-sided conversation.

She wore a Raaaaspberry Beret, the kind you find in a second-hand store...

Eventually we get past the weather and the fact it is Monday and 175 degrees outside. She allows me the grace of rinsing and before she can stick anything back in my mouth I ask her a question: "Candace, can I ask you what might be a strange question?"

"*Uh-huh.*"

"How did you decide to become a dental hygienist?"

By now, her kindness to and familiarity with my family has cut through my frustration about not writing. So I figure I would get some help for the book from her. Throughout the answer, her hands are holding blunt-force weapons assaulting my teeth, the ones that get flossed only every six months, by her. This requires her hands in my mouth again. The sound is horrific. So I try to concentrate on her answer.

"*I don't know...When I was a little girl, I was terrified*

of the dentist and threw up every time I had to go. The whole experience scared me. When I graduated from high school, I figured I had to do something. So I studied to do this."

This makes absolutely no sense to me. But I picture a room full of these chairs and young girls standing beside them nervously.

"I used to have this little boy who came to me. And he would throw up every single time he came. And we... I would never get to finish cleaning his teeth. One day I decided along with his mom, that we were gonna just clean him up and sit him right back down in this chair and finish. So we did. And he never threw up again. I suppose I'm doing this cause I know what it feels like to be scared of the dentist."

Let her cry, let her tears fall down like rain...

"I've been doing this here for 30 years now. I remember when your wife was a little girl and now she brings her children in here and her and I are friends on Facebook. That little boy who stopped being scared now brings his kids in here and I love to tell them about how scared their Daddy was. It helps."

She keeps on poking and prodding and drawing blood with a smile on her face.

Candace is a Christian and we have talked about church life and faith a good bit before. Actually she talks and I nod. If she had not been holding shiny sharp objects in my mouth I would've told her how glad I am she does what she does. When sin entered the world through Adam's Fall, along with it came death and pain.[1] Also, it ushered in plaque and tartar, cavities and abscesses, root canals and gums that get damaged. And children full of fear to the point that their stomachs do violence to the whole room.

Candace's hospitality, smiles, digital picture frames, and skills are pushing back Adam's Fall, day-in and day-out. When

---

1   Genesis 3 (ESV). Most Christians believe that when Eve and Adam ate from the Tree of the Knowledge of Good and Evil in the Garden of Eden, sin entered the world. Along with sin came not only alienation from God, but God's curse, which includes pain and suffering.

she wields those weapons of mouth destruction she is not just fighting gum disease and the need for a filling, she is fighting against the effects of sin. As a follower of the King, she is taking on all that wars against His rule and reign. And she does it with flavored fluoride.

I chose melon.

CHAPTER FIVE

The Wrong Story

The inner spaces that a good story lets us enter are the old apartments of religion.

John Updike

I was not much of a college student. Not because I was at parties or hung over. That was never my problem; I simply was incapable of doing the work assigned. An avid reader of everything except what was assigned in the class, I would read until all hours of the night convincing myself at various intervals, in myriad of ways, how I could escape the homework hanging over me like debt. And my worst classes were my English classes. Languishing, I could not write anything worth reading to save my life. And my attention was hard to keep. This was especially true of one particular assignment: we were supposed to write a paper on one of those Greek myths I can never remember the name of, where some god falls in love with a mortal and it ends badly. It did not matter what I wrote or how I wrote it. I read the wrong Greek myth. None of the questions could be answered because I had read the wrong story. My answers — the ones I turned in that day — were fulsome and showed a complete understanding of what I had read. My teacher congratulated me. But I failed. I failed because I read the wrong story.

We are reading the wrong story.

The story of what God has done has been replaced by the story of us. And it's a tragic comedy featuring all of what we have done and have not done. The wrong story yields the wrong answers. We look at our own story and see nothing spectacular. And we draw, like master artists, the conclusion of an inferior spirituality, Rembrandts all.

As I write this I'm realizing for the first time the category of "mundane" only exists in its relationship to other categories. If there were no category of "extraordinary," ordinary would have no meaning at all. So the category of extraordinary gets used, by our hearts, as a weapon against all that pales in comparison. And we wield it mercilessly.

Sometimes, we take other people's stories — their callings, exploits, adventures, and endeavors — and categorize ourselves accordingly, in contrast. It's foolish, but we cannot help ourselves. How could the banker compare to the pastor? And the homemaker to the missionary?

But this never really works, though it works on our insecurity, for there is always someone more ordinary and less significant than us in this economy.

It's the wrong story.

God's story helps. But not in the way we are apt to think. We read, "be holy as I am holy" and all is well.[1] We run aground, though, when we read of God's extraordinary-ness and then compare ourselves accordingly. Standing in this scale, we all are found wanting. Everyone is mundane compared to the God of the Universe. Comparing stories with God is a losing game. Now we are just reading the right story wrongly.

Typical. I can only assume followers of Jesus have been turning the story into a how-to manual for time out of mind. But it's *news*, not a ten-step program.

How do we read and hear the story of God rightly? How do we read this story so as to gain encouragement in the midst of living a mundane life? How does God's story help us lunge toward belief in a God of the mundane?

With gaping mouths and wide eyes. With open hands. With wonder. And from the beginning.

We start with the fact that in the beginning God created the heavens and the earth. Paul tells us much later that God created everything.[2] There is nothing He did not create. In other words, He created the mountains we travel thousands of miles to behold and every blade of grass we stand upon as we are

---

1 Lev 11:44; I Peter 1:16 (ESV).
2 Colossians 1:16 (ESV).

doing the beholding. The very miles we wish away on a long journey were wished into reality in his infinite wisdom. Every tree that falls unheard and the sequoias we can drive through. All flowers blooming unseen and those tenderly pruned in English gardens. The marble from which masterpieces are struck and the dirt we kick from our shoes without thinking. And the shoes, themselves. All of it created by God. All of it.

Speaking of gardens: the first vocation was Gardener.[3] Yet there are few vocations less-celebrated in our world.

"Wait a second," you say, "the first vocation was not full-time ministry? The first vocation was not a prophet or a preacher?" No, not a prophet or preacher, but someone who worked with their hands tending to the garden. Here we glimpse the God of the mundane at work: the God of gardeners and farmers, veterinarians and plumbers, landscape designers and zoo-keepers.

We are beginning to see something in this story.

Maybe Adam and Eve got a little bored with gardening and animal husbandry. Maybe they looked at God as they were walking in the cool of the day with Him and liked the eternality and authority in His story better. Maybe they wanted more than the mundane existence they had been given.

Regardless, they wanted to be like God. They did not want to be found in God's story so much as write a better one. So they fell headlong into the abyss of unbelief and hate and determined rebellion. And worse, they pulled us in by the heel. And we have not gone kicking and screaming like we should.

But God showed mercy. God shows mercy to gardeners, gardeners who hide from him, and pass the buck, and bring a curse on the very thing they were supposed to care for. In a dramatic foreshadowing of what will come soon enough, God kills some animals to provide the covering for Adam's shame and Eve's. I don't know for certain all the significance of what I am about to write but...

God's first act of mercy was toward a gardener.

And mercy? Though Adam dove headlong into death itself, the God-Man dove in after us. And this redemptive work has been done for "all who believe."[4]

---

3   Genesis 2:15 (ESV).
4   Romans 1:16 (ESV)

The Apostle Paul writes to the Corinthians what would be an insult in our culture: "none of you were noble or great. God chose the small and foolish and low and despised."[5] It is hard to read these words and not see God's heart for the mundane over against the extraordinary.

The story of what God has done, and is doing, and will do, is the story of an extraordinary God creating, and then dying for, all the mundane.

All this convinces me of one thing: there is a spirituality in the ordinary. There is a spirituality for ordinary people who live ordinary lives. Jesus did not die to change this so much as make it more so. We are not saved from mediocrity and obscurity, the ordinary and the mundane. We are saved in the midst of it. We are not redeemed from the mundane. We are redeemed from the slavery of thinking our mundane life is not enough.

---

5   I Corinthians 1:26-27 (ESV)

CHAPTER SIX

Of Pastors and Plumbers

Toiling, — rejoicing, — sorrowing,
Onward through life he goes;
Each morning sees some task begin,
Each evening sees its close;
Something attempted, something done,
Has earned a night's repose.

Henry Wadsworth Longfellow, "The Village Blacksmith"

We have this cat, and his name is Auburn University Redmond. We call him Aubie. That is, unless we are mad at him. Then the full name flies out of our mouths like bullets screaming for their marks.

That's happened a lot. Aubie has spent a lot of time in trouble. He has fought dogs, cats, and who knows what else. He has jumped from forty feet up, down to the ground, and then has run like the wind itself to hold counsel under the neighbor's house.

Yes, he has spent more time than his fair share at the vet.

Not too long ago, my wife had to take our wayward cat to spend some time with the vet. He had a lot of recommendations for medications, treatments, supplements and dietary changes. They are expensive and none were needed in the strictest sense of the word.

Now, I think our veterinarian is a nice man. And every single idea he had for the health of my cat came from his love for animals — for cats, even specifically my cat. And this is the problem.

My veterinarian — my cat's doctor — is more concerned about the cat than me. He did not become a doctor to animals because he cared about their owners. I've no doubt he cares about the owners, I'm just not sure that is his passion. So my guess is, he has a very specific vision for the health of my cat. But not really for my bank account.

Veterinarians care about only one specific part of the household: the pet part. Doctors are probably the same way, as well as lawyers, and accountants, and plumbers, and landscape architects, and interior designers. Plumbers aren't thinking, "well, if they get this cheap pipe they won't have great pipes but they *will* be able to afford to go out to eat this month."

Plumbers are passionate about piping and water flowing. Veterinarians are passionate about animal health. Farmers are passionate about vegetables. Lawyers are passionate about people having wills. The tendency is for all of us to have the expectation for everyone else to be passionate about what we are passionate about. We think that what is front and center for us should be front and center for everyone else.

Plumbers have trouble understanding why I don't worry much about water pressure. Veterinarians think I should care about animals more. Potato farmers think I should eat more potatoes. Lawyers think I should understand the law better.

And pastors think everyone is not passionate enough about their faith, like they are.

I know this because I am a pastor. And I have been one for years. My life revolves around studying the Bible, being at the church's meeting place, talking about theology, connecting all the dots for people, planning church events, and attending them and serving at them.

It took me years to realize that this is my life as a pastor and not the life of anyone else. The life of everyone else is very different. It is full of all those things we are tempted to label as mundane in the spiritual stratosphere. Sure, every Christian has to deal with these things to a degree, but they are not the rhythm of their day-in and day-out lives as it is for a pastor.

Of course, plumbers should care about the Bible and theology and what is going at their church. And it is good for them to have a desire to serve their congregation. But a pastor does all these things because he is a pastor. It is his vocation. A plumber makes sure our pipes are working and our toilets are flushing. It is his vocation — *his calling.*

But the problem is that sometimes we pastors tend to forget this. We forget our calling is different from the calling of those we teach and counsel. We push back against the effects of the Fall through the ministry of the word: through counseling and preaching, studying and leading.

Plumbers push back the effects of the Fall through fixing leaky pipes.

Teachers do it through making sure children learn how to count, and read, and write.

Bankers push against the Fall with safes and loans to small businesses.

Farmers, with combines and turn-rows.

Librarians, with organized shelves full of wonder and adventure and beauty.

Baristas, with coffee, muffins and smiles.

Cooks push back with Duck a L'orange, Chicken Massaman and pizza.

Homemakers, with clean floors and changed diapers and home-cooked meals.

Artists push back the Fall with songs and paintings and pictures and stories.

All of it is a pushing back of the Fall itself. When we, who are subjects of the King, live out His rule and reign wherever we are, we push against the insurrection of sin with all its corruption, lies, and ugliness.

But my tendency has always been to downplay *that* work and get my congregants to see it as only a means to an end. Why did they work? For the glory of God, of course. How did they glorify God in their work? By making money so as to fund the work of ministry and missions. Which sounded like, "You work so that I as a pastor can work." Where they worked also existed primarily to serve the work of evangelism. The work was a means to an end, and held no meaning itself.

Seasons of ministry surged by before I could grasp my job was not so simple. I could not simply tell these people what to do. I had to help them see how what they are doing is a reflection of God himself and then get them to push into it.

Murry was outstanding in almost everything. He was one of

those kids who just did everything well. You know, the kind you wanted to be like and also hated when you were a teenager. As a youth pastor, I found that by the time he got to a certain age, he became more of a friend than a student. One day we were talking over a meal and he told me he was thinking about becoming a youth pastor. Or a doctor.

The flattery of one of your students wanting to be what you are is overwhelming. For the life of me I cannot remember what I told him. But thankfully he is going to be a doctor. He will be a great doctor. He is brilliant and kind. And such brilliance and kindness will be a formidable force against the ravages of a world where sickness and death are inevitable realities.

This story rushes to the front of my mind often, because it is symbolic of much of what we get wrong as Christians. There was this part of me that wanted to hear him say he wanted to be in the ministry more than anything. To do what I do. It would have justified my work easily, and would have confirmed the work of the Spirit in his life. For it is a necessary requirement for all pastors to be believers. The same cannot be said for surgeons.

Maybe it's because we think disciples should look like pastors, when actually for the most part they look like everyone else.

This is easy for artists; they easily see that their work is spiritual in nature. There is something about poetry and song, painting and writing that reeks of religion. But plumbers do not need to hear that for them to be better Christian plumbers they need to be like their pastor. They need to be plumbers — better plumbers.

There has to be some significance to Jesus spending most of his life as a carpenter. Why didn't he start his public ministry earlier? Why spend so much time doing something so mundane as being a carpenter, working in a rural town with wood, and stones, and the materials?

Materials he fashioned in the beginning.

Did a Rabbi ever wonder if a 20-year-old Jesus should not be settling for such a mundane life as that of a carpenter? He most likely showed some promise in the field of theology and everything else.

We pay lip service to the idea that being a pastor is not more spiritual than being something else. But we do not really believe that. The pastor is tempted to think the businessman should be more like him in his study. And the businessman is tempted to think his work in the boardroom is not spiritual at all.

But every believing businessman, plumber and homemaker is given the Holy Spirit. And their work with the raw materials of this world is intrinsically spiritual, though seemingly mundane compared with the pastor's work.

Pastors need to know this and plumbers need to know this. Pastors need to know it so they encourage plumbers to be faithful plumbers. And plumbers need to know this so they can grow as a plumber and not think they must be something else.

CHAPTER SEVEN

The Sermon You've Never Heard

There is a strength of quiet endurance as significant of courage as the most daring feats of prowess.

Henry Tuckerman

My whole life has been churched. Church has marked the contours of most of my days since I was young. Whether we are talking about the buildings or the people, the story of my life could not be written without all the trappings of the Church in the American South. I am one of its products. I've been supported by pews in a multitude of cities, and I've preached and taught grace in some others. The number of sermons, good and bad, that I've heard must number on up into the thousands.

And my memory is pretty good.

But I have never heard a sermon calling me to live quietly. Not one. At least that I can remember. I've heard heaps of sermons on what I should watch, listen to, whom I should date/marry, and how I should treat them. I've heard sermons on sex and alcohol and tobacco. I've heard sermons calling me to be bold about sharing the gospel. And sermons about being a missionary overseas because their need of the gospel over there is great. Sermons telling me I need to be a missionary here. And the all-Christians-are-missionaries-sermons I've heard preached could choke a horse, one of those horses in the Budweiser commercials.

(If all Christians are missionaries how come plumbers never speak at missions conferences?)

And I've heard sermons about not worrying what other people think when I witness to them. And sermons, preached with wild eyes, calling us to a life of radical morality and missional living.

But I've never heard a sermon asking me to have a quiet life. Or if I have, I've forgotten it and it's been lost over time under an avalanche of one hundred sermons on everything else.

In 1 Thessalonians 4:11 (ESV), Paul urges his hearers "to aspire to live quietly." And in 2 Thessalonians 3:12 he encourages them "in the Lord Jesus Christ to do their work quietly." But I've never heard a sermon on what he means by "quiet" or "quietly." Or what he means by "live" or "life." I've heard many how-to sermons but none on how to live quietly, and what it might look like in our culture, which is so loud about everything.

How do you live quietly with three kids, eight and under?

Paul isn't just suggesting this to the Thessalonians. He is *urging* them to live quietly. Wait a second — no, he wants these believers to *aspire* to live quietly. You could translate these words as "make it your ambition to live quietly." This is no small thing. And this quiet living is important enough for him to include it in both letters to the Thessalonian Christians. And he wants Timothy to give the same instructions to his people.

It is hard to make a splash in the world when we are living quietly. A quiet life will put us out of the way of attention. There are things we have to be quiet about. We would need to recede into the shadows of this world. Step back. We would have to keep things to ourselves for a change.

I bring all this up because *quiet* fits with this idea of being mundane. The mundane life is one where we quietly go about our business. No easy task. Which is why Paul commands it of us.

Commentaries are funny. Whenever I read one about these verses, the commentary writer feels the need to make sure we understand Paul is not asking us to stop being bold in our witness. When did he *start* asking us? It's puzzling that although we see evidence of disciples preaching before hostile crowds, being beaten and even executed, we are never actually commanded to be bold in our witness.

Why would first-century Christians, who felt the threat of persecution more keenly than us, have a hard time being quiet about their faith? Wouldn't we expect Paul to push them towards boldness at every turn? But Paul never calls them to live as missionaries and do evangelism every time they go to the market or see their neighbor.

This is all so weird. Backwards, even.

It is true that the call to evangelize comes in the great commission. But I do wonder why Paul does not reiterate that call. Hard to say. What is undeniable is the lack of imperatives to evangelize and the clear call to live quietly. This does not preclude evangelism by any means. But maybe we should do more than glance at these strange (at least to us) calls to live quietly.

Paul calls the Thessalonians to live quietly and never commands them to evangelize. Whereas, we call people to be bold and not worry about offending people in our call to evangelize. We are prone to think (and say) those who aspire to live quietly are carnal.

But Paul calls them to a life we would call "mundane" or "ordinary," while we call everyone to shift the world's axis. Can you imagine a conference for young people on "living quietly"? Hard to do. However, it is easy to imagine one filled with instructions on how to turn the world upside down. With plenty of imagination to spare.

Why? One answer is that we have no vision for what is commonly thought of as mundane. And quiet is mundane. Boring. In our spiritual economy, quiet is of no worth. It has no real cash value. So, no real investment in such a venture can be expected.

I'm partly to blame.

Though I've stood before people preaching and teaching, literally a thousand times, I've never taught on this passage. And the reason is simple. As a preacher, you want to motivate people out of ordinary life to do things. And to stop doing things. But mostly, you just want them to do really big, important things for Jesus. You want them to do things they can see and you, the motivator, can see. Significance in influence's clothing.

Quiet is the opposite of extraordinary. How can we be a

bold witness for Christ if we are quiet? I made a living out of telling students to be bold in class about their morals and doctrines, their convictions and beliefs.

Why? Because it was something they could latch onto. It has big brass handles and they could easily take such teaching home with them, and into the streets, and classrooms, and parties, and locker rooms.

So what might a sermon or lesson on the aspiration to live quietly look like? I would make sure the people before me heard two things in particular.

First, we need to get our heads around the fact this little teaching is the polar opposite of not only the way the unbelieving world does things but also the way the majority of Christendom goes about its business.

The world around us is formed by celebrity and self-promotion. We are anxious to tell everyone what we love, what we are fans of, what we have done, and what we will be doing. We are quick to assert what we like and don't like. Not to mention who we know. And the louder we are the more others hear and know.

And the Church is no different. We believe we cannot just go about our business. We must broadcast it so people will look at us, our church, our denomination. *Our* works. The flesh is the reason. We are suffering from its poison coursing through our veins.

Eve and Adam should have just been quiet in the face of the serpent.

Walking away is one way to be quiet. But this is the world of protest. Public denunciations and PR campaigns define us. And what is good for the world is good for the Church. Or so we think.

Think about it. This living quietly is not only ignored in the Church, it is rarely if ever seen as faithfulness. Not in *this* culture where the quiet is anathema. We Christians need to reckon with the fact our tendency to not see a quiet/mundane life as legitimately spiritual comes from pride, a pride betrayed when we cannot be quiet about what we have done, and suffered, and seen. Ever.

Second, quiet is not just about volume. It's about tone and

spirit. It's not only what we don't say. It is all of life we are talking about here: a life of contentment, a life of more thought than speech, more thought *before* speech. Living quietly is a life so happy with the attention of God, that the attention of the world is not needed, and rarely enjoyed.

Fifteen minutes of fame is too short for the one who enjoys the security of fellowship with the King.

This is not a monk's venture. This is not silence. I think more than anything it is the resolve to be okay in not being heard, or seen, or noticed. It is grounded in the assurance of the notice of the Creator. The quiet life — just like the mundane life — is not weak. It is the strength of the Lamb who stood silent before his slaughterers.

This needs to be heard. It is no irony. In a world of blogs, status updates, social media and digitalized narcissism, the church needs to hear the whispered call to a holy ambition of living quietly in the world where the corners of it are despised and rejected.

CHAPTER EIGHT

"God's Special Moment"

Above me to the left are framed black-and-white photos of my hometown: kids swimming in community pools, the old terminal station long torn down. Steel mills are the subject of every other captured moment, now gone. They cover a wall in a restaurant I remember eating at as a kid. This *was* a barbecue joint, one still firmly fixed in the minds of those my age and older.

There are blooms of Hydrangea in Coke-bottle vases on each table.

My corner spot allows me to look over the place, which is spic-and-span. On the other side of the windows in front of me and across the street, I can see a train. The cars, covered in rust and graffiti, wait to make their way into the valley holding downtown Birmingham in mountainous arms. I can feel the train moving along the tracks. Behind me is the interstate, a critical artery, clogged like one after a lifetime of casseroles and fried chicken. And fried pickles.

Fifty years ago this building bustled. Thankfully, it does so still.

Now most of the space not used for cooking is set up for a church's worship service. But I'm in the comfortable and welcoming, soft-piano-music part branded as the "Kairos Kafe." Their main business is "Katering" but the Kafe is open for lunch.

They said I could sit here and write until they close up. By the look on the hostess's face, I could tell I was the only person they had ever encountered who was glad they had no wi-fi.

To my left is a "bar," where they dispense soft drinks and to-go menus. The only alcohol winked at is a white wine sauce for a chicken dish. On the wall above this faux bar is a sign made to look as if the paint has been peeled back to reveal a dictionary definition of "kairos," long lost. This tells us how to pronounce the word and alerts us to its Greek origin. The principal definition is "God's special moment," a definition followed by "time" and "the critical moment". As a student of Greek, I know the first does not land square but is close enough to the Scriptures' intended meaning.

I wonder how many people think a really good lunch is "God's special moment." You know, besides myself.

In a city awash in Greek and Mediterranean restaurants, you'd think this is yet another of such genus. But the biggest part of their menu is Chicken Tenderloins. In the cultural pool I swim in, these are chicken fingers. They seem to be famous for them, whether grilled or fried. To have a good reputation for these — in a city right smack dab in the middle of Dixie — says something. There are no restaurants in this city without chicken fingers on the menu. We not only think of them as a staple but as a delicacy.

This is our *foie gras*.

Southern Fried Broccoli is on the menu. Even the thought of such a thing deserves a Nobel Prize for Culinary Art.

There is nothing that is not incredible. I assault my meal with abandon.

I'm sitting here at the corner table alone, but I am not alone. The waitresses and hostess constantly check on me with happy faces. They seem glad to work here. And when they ask if I like my food, I gush, "It. Is. Incredible." They agree with a warm, whispery, "I know!" As if it were indiscreet for us all to agree on this certifiable fact.

I may be the only one in the room not drinking sweet tea.

Their mission statement is "building relationships around food." The words, large and prominent, greet you as you make your way across the pavement.

I asked James, the owner, about it.

Our mission statement "building relationships around food" came to my Katering director, Jeremy, when we were opening Kairos and throwing around ideas for a mission statement. We had several in mind but this one stuck because it was so simple, and exactly what I wanted Kairos to achieve. I made up my mind that it was perfect after I planned to frame my first dollar and hang it up over the register. It was really neat what I felt like God said to me: "James, don't hang up your first dollar, because Kairos will be about the people, not about the money." So, I never knew where our first dollar went. Instead, I took a picture of the first customers and hung that up instead. Over the past five years it has been an awesome journey building relationships around food, not only with my customers, but with my staff, and others who need some direction in life.

This is not just marketing. And it's not only Southern hospitality.

This is the faithfulness of ordinary work. Which consequently has the air of being more than mundane when that air is full of the aroma of great food wafting through.

This is faithfulness working itself out of a heart full of love for people (workers and customers) and homemade food. Two everyday things God has given, coming together every day. For folks around here, at the very least three times a day.

They should be open for all three.

CHAPTER NINE

No One Wants to be George Bailey

You will be like God.

Satan

There is a scene in *It's A Wonderful Life*, the classic film about someone who made a difference without even knowing it, in which George Bailey wants to buy a suitcase. Excited, he tells the salesman, "I don't want something for one night, I want something for a thousand and one nights!" The salesman shows him a secondhand piece of luggage and George likes it. There is plenty of space for stickers from all the places he will go and see. He asks how much it is.

"No charge."

"That's my trick ear, Joe. It sounded as if you said no charge."

But he heard right: "old man Gower," his old boss, bought it for him. If I close my eyes, I am sitting on the brown couch, itself sitting on shag carpet of three shades of green in what was once my den, and I can see and hear George say, "he did?!" And then he heads over to the drugstore old man Gower owns, where George used to work.

This is a powerful scene. I have watched this movie more than any other movie and I cannot help but think this is the most meaningful scene in the whole film. Here we have George bursting with excitement and on the edge of adventure. We are thrilled with him. But only the first time we watch the film.

For now we know.

We know the torment that is coming. We know he must

43

shelve his trip because of his father's death. And then he will once again be disappointed, watching his dreams shatter on the craggy rocks of reality. His brother Harry will not be coming home to take the reins of the family business, the Bailey Building and Loan.

Another scene: he is standing outside of his home. Inside is a celebration of his brother's marriage. He has had to feign joy while harboring defeat. Before his mother comes out to push him in the direction of Mary Hatch's home, we watch him look with distress at the brochures representing his dreams of leaving behind the mundane life he leads in Bedford Falls. And Jimmy Stewart, in a beautiful piece of acting, tosses those dreams of escape and adventure away, and the brochures are thrown on the ground, only to be trod upon by those who could never know his disappointment.

And it's not over. Another scene: he is now married to Mary Hatch. They have a triumphant handful of cash and are on their way out of town in Bert's taxi. They are on the edge of a dream honeymoon. Not only is George Bailey about to escape the mundanity of his hometown — the only environs he has known — but he is about to leave with his new wife. But again the dream is squelched and he, in a gorgeous moment, uses his own money meant for his honeymoon to save the business he runs and cares for. The life he pictured has once again been thrown to the threshing floor where things beyond his control deal mercilessly with his dreams.

Everyone focuses on the end of this movie. In the end we can see George's life was used to help people. And not only does he change the lives of people in his town, but the effects of his everyday decisions, starting in childhood, reverberate with significance throughout the world. He realizes this because heaven has entered into his life in the form of an angel named Clarence. He has finally seen what he has accomplished in the midst of such a mundane existence. And so, on the verge of taking his own life, joy and a new zeal for life take over. Everyone loves this part of the movie, as do I.

The end of the picture is when we get God's perspective, of course. Heaven has burst in and George is now able to see clearly. We see clearly. Previously we all saw in a glass darkly, but now, clear. We like this. For we want to be the George Bailey whose significance has been revealed. However, we do not want to be the George Bailey who leads a mundane life, void of the excitement of the wider world which he longed for. We identify with his frustrations. We run away from the mundane. Or we tolerate it in expectation of something...other. Wanting to have the same kind of impact on people's lives is not the same as wanting to be George Bailey. No one really wants to be George Bailey.

The movie is profound on a level we rarely ever operate on. Let's look at another scene. George is about to jump from a bridge into the river, but Clarence (the angel) jumps in first because he knows George's character and history, and knows George will then jump in to save him. They are now sitting in a building by the river. The snow is blowing outside, but it is warm inside by the stove. George's clothes are now drying out. Our suicidal subject is lamenting his life and Clarence utters the very statement summing up the message of the movie. He says, "you just don't know all that you've done."

All his dreams are crashing around him and George is staring straight in the face of the horrific idea that he has done nothing in his life. We get this, don't we? No one wants to grow up and be a nobody who lived a mundane life. We want to be rock stars. We want to be the kind of people books get written about. We want to leave our mark on the world. Obscurity is rarely the stuff of daydreams. Since the only people we celebrate are celebrities (singers, actors, writers, and, in the church, celebrity pastors and biography-worthy missionaries) we of course want to be worthy of such talk ourselves. And this is what we want for our kids: to be celebrities. Not George Baileys.

We don't dream of being cashiers and clerks, toiling away in obscurity without notice of the wider world. A quiet and peaceful life where nothing of significance can be seen with the naked eye tends to be disdained inside and outside the church.

Christians could learn a lot here. We are guilty of not knowing what all we have done. But actually, that is not where the real guilt lies, even if it is where we feel it. The actual guilt lies in our thinking because we do not know all that we have done, we must have done nothing. We assume some kind of godlike posture as if we know the ends and implications of all our actions, and then we make judgments based on them. Foolish, isn't it — this idea we have no significance because we have not seen it? We wallow in some kind of faux humility, never realizing it is really ego that thinks, "If I cannot see it, it must not be there."

If there's no place in the halls of heroic Christian faith for unknown housewives and clerks, then we are believing wrongly. Most people live mundane lives that will never be remembered beyond a couple generations, and only then by their family members. This can be painful. Every Christian wants to do something wonderful in the name of Jesus. And to come to the end of our rope or life, and not see that we did anything at all worthy enough to be called significant can be devastating.

Of course, it's a lie. And it's a lie if only because the two greatest commands Jesus gave are more often than not going to look very mundane: often our loving God will not be noticed and loving our neighbor will not be remembered. Sometimes they may be, but more often than not, forgettable and forgotten. But it is also a lie simply because we do not know. Who could know the effects of daily living out of the deep-end-of-the-pool belief in the killed and risen God for those who rebelled against him?

Since we cannot see that in our day-in and day-out faithfulness to God, we are accomplishing something, we then begin to re-evaluate our lives. We think: "I cannot see I have done anything at all with my life. Therefore I must do something significant." So we then go into the ministry. Or do something with the promise of giving us the immediate satisfaction of seeing significance done. Finished. And done by us.

This is not to say we should never take stock of what our lives are made up of. But we must face the fact there is a latent arrogance in this line of thinking: the arrogance of presumed omniscience. The arrogance of needing immediacy for validation. The problem is this does not look anything like the conceit we are acquainted with. This looks like ambition and single-mindedness, two virtues that make great leaders.

However, this is not all.

There is a third stage. And it is the worst of all. Stage one: I feel guilty about doing nothing. Stage two: therefore I must get on with something obviously significant.

Stage three: now we judge others by this standard.

If they are not doing something obviously significant then we automatically say to ourselves or to them and certainly to others, "they are not serious about their faith! If they were, they would do..."

And now as if there is not enough in the Scriptures given to us by God, we churn out new laws — in this case, the law of "do something big" — to prop up our own righteousness and judge another's by. All hope is now located in what we are doing that is so wonderful for God.

And it all started with the very first lie, "you will be like God, knowing..."[1]

A huge part of all this is the belief that nothing so mundane as wanting to "live quietly" can be significant. The idea that God can take the seemingly small, mundane tasks and responsibilities and turn them into something significant, while a strange way of thinking for us, is a common thread divinely woven throughout the Scriptures: shepherds watching their flocks by night, an old couple finally having children, a little boy's lunch of bread and fish.

This is crucial. Not only have we forgotten the hope and assurance of the grace given to us by trading it in for "significant" works, but we have forgotten the very content of the story.

We should be the people most willing to buy into the view of life that sees work and making babies and caring for them as significant. These, after all, are what we were originally created and called to be doing.[2] When we watch the lives of George Baileys lived out in front us, frustrated and tempted to think they have done little, we ought to be the representatives of the Kingdom most anxious to comfort them with, "you just don't know all that you've done!"

---

1 Genesis 3:5 (ESV).
2 Genesis 1:28 (ESV).

CHAPTER TEN

The Gospel of Something Else Entirely

Everybody's working for the weekend.

Loverboy

I t's early in the week and all you can do is wait for the weekend to get here.

Well, it's not all you can do. You can daydream and plan and tell others about the awesome plans you have made. You can trudge through the mundane job before you, with the hope of something better to come, whether it be the lake, the beach, a date, or a night out with friends.

This is how we live our weeks. Ease of labor is made possible by the promise of a break from it. Monday through Friday we walk through the valley of the shadow of work and school. When Friday comes, we enjoy the good news of the clock, world without end. Until then, we manage by enjoying happy hours, long lunches, and a good film, but we want something else entirely different from the work week.

And we most likely have a spirituality in the same vein. We eagerly await doing spiritual things and being involved with spiritual enterprises. We look to the future. We look away to something outside of what we are doing. Regardless of where we are and what we happen to be doing, we must wait for something else or be somewhere else to have a spiritually significant moment.

That moment is here, but we are believing the gospel of something else entirely.

And this is understandable, because the gospel is, in fact, something else entirely. It is entirely outside of our opinions, for the good news of the Kingdom is out there regardless of our belief in it. Also, it is a message of God working, and rescuing, and changing us, because we cannot do it ourselves.

But there is also a problem here. The "gospel of something else entirely" steals the significance of here and now. Now gives way to later. Here loses out to there. The present moment and the place where that moment passed are labeled insignificant.

I buy the bread for communion. And I buy it from a big-box store on my way to where our church meets on Sunday mornings. It is easy for me to focus on the fact I am getting bread for communion, which will take place a few hours later than when I buy it. What is not easy for me to focus on are the moments strung together as I am buying the loaf of bread. How do I respond to and think about the sleepy greeter who barely acknowledges my existence as I enter the store? Am I thankful for the cool air of the store? Do I stand in wonder at all the food before me? Do I long for everyone to get the heck out of my way so I can get there? Get there. There is where the importance lies.

This is no call for navel-gazing guilt. What I am after is a life of moment-by-moment significance. I'm after the good news of the Mark 1:15 sort.[1] The Kingdom of God is at hand. I am part of this Kingdom. I am not waiting to be part of it when I die. I am not more a part of it when I am in church listening to a sermon or eating this bread. When I buy the bread — any bread — I am involved in transactions that are Kingdom transactions.

This changes everything. No longer is the gospel the promise of something else entirely. It is now the message of *now*. Now you are redeemed. Now you are living as a member of the Kingdom. You are disciplining your child, taking a bath, paying bills, and cutting grass as a member of the Kingdom of God and of his Christ. And the reason this changes everything is because everything is now part of this life in the Kingdom.

---

1   ..."The time is fulfilled, and the kingdom of God is at hand; repent and believe in the gospel." (ESV)

Every mundane moment sitting uncomfortably between those of ecstasy, spiritual or otherwise is now worthy of attention. It is no longer necessary to live on the fumes of the spiritual high that was, or look forward to a future hit. We have now the fellowship of the King. Every act is now of Kingdom consequence.

Not just the big ones.

Sure, there will be times when "getting this" will be like finding needles in haystacks or pulling teeth. But this is when I think the message of the gospel for now — this moment — is singularly good news. It does not only offer promises of the future but holds out promise for now — even now when we cannot see the goodness of the news — it is still present. We are still loved by the King.

If it is true that the Kingdom is at hand then we had better get rid of the "gospel of something else entirely." The gospel of "going to heaven and not hell" and the gospel of "feeling great while listening to sermons and worship songs" is woefully inadequate.

I agree, it is great news: we, followers of Jesus, are not going to hell and instead are promised a glorious eternal existence. And I've nothing against enjoying sermons and worship songs... well, some worship songs. But one is a gospel dealing with only later, and the other leaves us in the position of experiencing the indwelling presence of our God at church or if we have our headphones handy. What about now? While we are eating with our families? Sitting in the library? Mopping the floor? Doing homework? Shopping for a new belt?

When people would walk away from the Christian faith, I used to find it odd. And it is still compelling and lovely enough for me to be astonished. However, now I do wonder. I wonder why they would stay if the faith they are adhering to is all about something else entirely. Oh, our faith can be about now, if we give our lives to Jesus fully and go oversees to tell others about Him. Or go into full-time ministry as a pastor. But, if we are a banker, or doctor, or a barista, well, we only get Sundays (maybe Wednesday nights), the drive home if we listen to Christian music, and the annual missions trip. But there is nothing for the bulk of our lives. They are unspiritual, which must mean they are devoid of the Spirit of Christ, our King — our Savior. Our friend. What happened to all the good news? A life of millions of millions of moments that are of no consequence is terrible news.

I advise no one to walk away. But what I do advise is a rejection of the gospel of something else entirely — the gospel that has nothing to do with all the times and places which are not typically called "spiritual." I enthusiastically advise a rejection of any gospel that demeans the day-in and day-out labors of homemakers, who must vacuum the Cheerios out of the sofa, courtesy of the resident toddler, by suggesting such a thing is not of eternal consequence. When in fact, they are pushing back the effects of Adam's Fall, itself.

CHAPTER ELEVEN

The Myth of An Easy Life

Be kind, for everyone you meet is fighting a hard battle.

Plato

In October of '96 I had a fairly serious car wreck. The difference of a few inches not only kept me alive, but preserved my sight: if my face had hit the windshield only slightly to one side or the other, I might not have the ability to see. If I close my eyes I can remember getting out of the car I had just paid off. I can remember looking down to see the warm blood streaming off my face onto my brown hiking boots. A few ladies from homes nearby ran out to help me. I remember sitting down quickly.

It would take months — years, really — to know the varied ways this event affected me. There were the obvious results. I was zealous to wear a seatbelt, which I had neglected to do. I bought a "new" used car, so I had a car payment again. And when I looked in the mirror, I had a face that was only vaguely familiar to me. There were scars and stitches everywhere. Bandages were sheepishly worn for weeks. To this day, if I am blinded by the sun while driving, I panic.

It took much longer than I expected, to deal with the emotional trauma of being close to death and wearing bandages and knowing people were looking at the scars scattered over my face. Just a few years ago, I reached up to scratch my forehead and the eyes of the person I was talking with widened. The cause revealed itself: I could feel the blood trickle down my forehead caused by glass making an untimely exit. Glass from the windshield of an '87 Honda Civic is still residing just below the surface as I type. Fifteen years later.

I didn't understand how such an event could affect me in so many little ways, all these years later.

In the same way, sometimes I wonder if we really understand how sinful our sin is. Sure, we get the fact our sin is all-out rebellion against the sovereign God of the universe. We know we have virtually stuck a fist in the face of the Father, called him an SOB, and then asked for the keys so we can leave home. We are even well aware of what it cost to deal with our sin problem: the killing of the Son. But for the most part, it seems that we are practically ignorant of the extent of our sin and its moment-by-moment effects.

To some degree, this is part of the grace we enjoy. We acknowledge how good it is when others cannot see those dark and dusty corners of our heart. But it is also a gracious thing to be shielded from the unfathomable depth of deadly treachery residing right inside of us. We thankfully cannot see it as it is. I, for one, am glad of this. The truth would overwhelm us, perhaps no less than the purity of the Father's glory revealed in all its splendor. We can't handle it.

However, we should still try to know ourselves enough to recognize that even on our best days, we are shot through with this thing called sin. Total depravity? Sure, whatever you want to call it. We are dealing with something that is not flat. Our sin problem has contours we will never even know. We will, for the rest of our earthly lives, be thoroughly ignorant of the extent of our sinfulness. There are outworkings of our sinfulness, particular to our culture, that we have not even been able to recognize yet. And there are some sins we will never even get a handle on. We may make progress, but even that will be tough. This is a lifelong project. But it is of the utmost importance to know that every facet of our lives has been compromised by rebellion.

I'm of the opinion that our ignorance of this and the particular way this truth manifests itself in our own lives is why we cannot see the God of the mundane. Beholding the God of martyred missionaries is easy. Discerning the God of the ascetic who has refused all temporal comforts is a piece of cake. But perceiving the God of those whose days are marked by the number of diapers changed is remarkably hard. The prevailing view of spirituality leaves us with ten thousand moments void of the glorious God. He is present when we do things like pray, read our Bible, sing worship songs, give away our stuff, and go overseas. But he is strikingly absent when we are doing mundane paperwork in Godforsaken cubicles of lifeless grey.

We have forgotten if we ever knew those words, "be kind, for everyone you meet is fighting a hard battle." Maybe we have not forgotten to be kind, but do we forget everyone is fighting a hard battle?

Not only are we having to deal with sin, but even the most mundane life is interrupted by disease, hardship, loneliness, fear, anxiety, nerves, instability, cancer, diabetes, glaucoma, poverty, broken bones, chronic migraines, bad backs, tornadoes, e-coli, colic, croup, heart disease, and the deaths of those we love. It is not just sin we must all deal with. We must deal with the *effects* of Adam's sin and our own — our fallen condition.

If we only knew that even when we are doing paperwork, and changing diapers, the reality of our own sin vying for control, we would not be so quick to think these mundane exercises are small in the spiritual stratosphere. All those mundane moments — the seconds turning into minutes, snowballing into hours between all the so-called spiritual exercises — are really infinite moments occupied by not only our blackened hearts but the Spirit of God working out what is pleasing to the Father.

And some want to call the Christian life easy.

At the moment, my family and I live just outside of a town called Mountain Brook. It huddles next to Birmingham on the south side of Red Mountain. The place is idyllic, full of natural beauty and that of the constructed sort. Many dream of living off Euclid so they can walk to La Paz or the local Thai restaurant in Crestline Village. It is truly a beautiful place full of beautiful people. And it has a stunning library full of mission-style furniture. Chairs for the soul.

But we forget our theology if we think living as a Christian would be easy in such a place. The very sin that courses through my soul-veins is present there. For me, or anyone else to think sin is more potent there betrays jealousy. Yet for me to think life is just easy there betrays rank foolishness. Every lavish home contains people who have seen disease. Every lawn that must be maintained is attached to a marriage that also must be maintained. Every street knows failure and tragedy, and no one, even if they have a pool house, is exempt from the demands of death. Money may stay the inevitable for a time, but no one can hold against that destiny which we all must reckon with.

I write none of this to excuse the wealth of others. I've so little wealth to excuse, that charge would fall flat if leveled. My point is if we knew how difficult the Christian life was — is — we would certainly not suppose that another life, with more spiritual parts to it, would be, well, more spiritual. We would see the gravity of living out our belief on our street, in stores, among our friends, before our servers at restaurants, and wherever we play. We think there are places where faith, and spirituality, and Christianity are easy. Some places may be harder. Maybe. But easy? We do not know ourselves, or the world around us very well if we think so.

CHAPTER TWELVE

"As Hard As It Is"

My wife and I are on the way to the beach for a short vacation sans kids. Twenty minutes into the trip the silence has all the glorious weight of Fort Knox gold. We are reveling in the lack of requests from the backseat when she gets a text from her friend, Missy.

> Just spent an hour filling up the plastic pool, applying sunscreen to 4 kids, putting on suits only to get in the pool for 4 seconds and then have 3 of the kids scream bc it's too cold!! Ha! Enjoy ur kidless trip!!

My wife and her friend do this often. Sharing their failures and laughing along with the other's is some kind of twisted, beautiful catharsis. Her husband, Sean, and I text about sports, music, and bacon.

The first time I met Missy, she introduced herself as "Matt." It took her a few moments to realize what she had done. No one laughed harder than she did.

Missy is mommy to four little ones, all seven and under. If it's OK for me to have a favorite of my friends' kids, it's their Ben.

When I ask Missy why they adopted Ben, the story is layered. Honest. Devoid of pretension. And you need to hear her nearly unedited voice, the voice my wife hears regularly:

To: Matt
From: Missy
Subject: why we adopted Ben

My first thought is just that I always knew I wanted to adopt. Just always drawn to it. I know that's not a good answer..but it's true. It was never because I thought we wouldn't be able to get pregnant. And I loved the idea of having different races in my family... kind of going against the "norm." I never thought of it as us "saving" a child. I think we went into it with just the hopes of adding another child to our family and we knew that there were kids out there that needed families too. I probably filled out 10 applications before we actually went through with it.

We never knew how hard it would be. I mean, we didn't think it would be easy, but I think we then thought it would eventually be "normal."

We are just now learning that life with an adopted child is just always going to be a little bit different. We are constantly worrying about all his behaviors.

"Are they normal for him?"

"Does this behavior mean he has an attachment problem."

"Does this behavior mean he has something wrong."

"Things we wouldn't necessarily think twice about with a biological child."

It feels lonely sometimes because you feel like you are trying to "make things wrong" with your child... because no one else really sees it... and it's hard... you can easily just pretend that everything is ok. I think after having him home for 5 years, I'm just now realizing this. I've tried to just make him be "normal", but he might just be different… and that is going to have to be ok. He might always be a little bit anxious. He might always have some learning issues. He might always have a hard time adjusting to change. But it is hard.

It's not all glamorous like some make you think it is. This is weird, but I always think about Brad and Angelina and wonder what kind of issues their kids have... but you never see that on tv. You always just see this "super cool multi-cultural family." But I always want to know what issues they face because those are the things that adoptive parents need to know.

I asked Missy about the difficulties of being a stay-at-home mom. Her answer is all at once humbling and hilarious.

To: Matt
From: Missy
Subject: RE: what are the difficulties?

The Difficulties? Everything.

Feeling like you are doing the same thing everyday and saying the
same thing a million times. Cleaning up the same toys everyday
(every hour). Pee on the bathroom floor. Trying to read a book over
a screaming child. Constantly breaking up fights or trying to get
them to get along. Teaching them things they don't understand..
I think I've made one cry almost every time I try to help him with
math homework. And even when you try to do something "good", it
doesn't go as planned (reading the bible story each night... usually
ends in frustration because no one is listening). Trying to find time
to THINK, or read, or finish a thought. Just finding the time to do
anything you want or need to do (exercise). Making four bowls of
cereal for breakfast and four cups of juice, and then the same for
lunch and dinner and then the millions of snacks each day.

I mean, it's hard. It's hard because you feel guilty when you aren't
doing something with the kids, and you feel guilty when you get
upset with them, and you feel like you are not teaching them the
things you really want to be teaching them..like how to be patient
and forgive and love each other. The endless piles of laundry. And
you know you are going to have to do it all again tomorrow!

What about the joys?

When your son asks you questions like "Mom, where did daddy
find you?"

"I want to be a daddy one day too!"

Or "mom, I prayed for you at school today."

And you get to hear all the funny stories. You get to see when they
actually do learn something. You are the one that is with them
all day and you get to listen to them and play and see the good
moments mixed in with the bad ones.

As hard as it is, I really would not change it.

And having friends struggling along with you helps you to know
you aren't crazy and that you aren't the only mom who screams or
gets upset or worried.

I think my list of difficulties was longer than the joys, but I don't
mean it to be. The joys seem self explanatory... you are WITH your
kids. It's just hard to be with them sometimes!

My guess? Missy's voice is the gut-felt echo from a chorus
of mothers stretching across the width and breadth of this cul-

ture.

Think about it: the homemaker may be the prototype of the mundane life. Every day is full of what the next day holds. And every day is filigreed with wondering if any of what is done is helping or hurting. Yet there are moments of happiness and the joy is real.

But the temptation to doubt if they are doing anything of significance is real.

"Does this matter?"

The temptation to question God's faithfulness is strong.

"Is God working in my child's life?"

"Is God working in my life?"

Missy would be the last to tell us her story is the standard by which any mom should measure herself. And she would most likely be the first to say she is just an ordinary wife and mom trying to be faithful with the life she has been given.

What will forever be known as the The Gloriously Quiet Vacation of 2011 is now over. Before I could finish this chapter, my wife sent me a text telling me that when she pumped up the pool, she ran down the van's battery. And the kids cannot understand after waiting all day why they cannot get in yet. I made sure she told Missy.

They'll laugh until they cry.

CHAPTER THIRTEEN

Mundane Kindness

*Whoever gives one of these little ones even a cup of cold water
because he is my disciple, truly, I say to you, he will by no
means lose his reward.*

Matt. 10:42 (ESV)

I'm well aware it is cooler to write in a cafe. But I like writing in the library. It's full of all kinds of people. Beautiful and ugly people, students and little tikes are in search of books. Soccer moms and hipsters reach out to the shelf in hope of a great read. And there are those looking for jobs, sculpting resumes and making use of free internet access.

I used to sit in this really comfortable chair. Used to, because it is too hard to get out of when done. And I once fell asleep while reading in it. This chair just happens to be situated right in front of a shelf frequented by women. The Christian fiction phenomenon of Amish romance is alive and well, I tell you, and those seeking it out have worn out the carpet in front of me. There is pretty much always a soccer mom standing a few feet from me, trying to decide which series of rebellious Amish-teenage-pregnant girls she will run through in the next 24 hours.

Usually, I am pretty much ignored unless someone I know happens upon my little corner.

However, one day, something memorable happened — memorable because it was different. It was the kind of thing that if you told me it would be memorable, I would wonder what you were getting at.

Some lady smiled at me.

And it was not the smile that says, "we have looked at

each other and I am acknowledging this fact." You know, that smile which is really no smile, where you pull in your lips and nod your head. There was nothing particularly sly about her smile. It contained no eros. And there was no reserve behind it. It lacked any pretension and seemed generous. Though I cannot understand why it was given, after thinking about this moment, kindness seems to be the only explanation I can come up with.

It was just a moment of kindness. That's all.

The reader, especially of the Southern sort, may be thinking, "why is this such a big deal?" Let me begin by pointing out, being smiled at, by strangers, is not unique in the South. I live in Alabama. We are famous for this kind of thing. We smile at strangers speeding past at 70 miles per hour. We smile while being routinely abused at the DMV.

Maybe it is not a big deal. But it didn't have the feel of social convention.

Here's the thing, I had no need for the smile. My week was going great. My wife was and is full of smiles for me. We laugh and smile with each other and our children throughout the day. There is no shortage of kindness expressed through smiles in our home. And the same is true among extended family. And friends. So it is not as if I was sulking in my chair, laboring away in gloom and was refreshed by a moment of kindness.

But let's suppose I am someone else.

Suppose I am someone else, sitting in a comfortable chair because I've no place of comfort to call my own.

Suppose I am a lifelong citizen in a world of hurt, when the smile leaps out of a life of kindness and lands on me. I have lost my job and I am laboring to scale the smooth, hard face of unemployment while feeding, clothing and sheltering a family. The library has free internet, so I can search for a job online.

I am a day removed from getting the news I have cancer. Or I have just found out my child has leukemia. A parent has passed away. A friend has lied to me. I am alone.

I have no one. Wandering this world, my interaction with others is limited to the goods and services I purchase.

Such a smile might be the lone drip of water in a desert.

Or an oasis.

Maybe we could call it "even a cup of cold water" for those thirsty for some kind, any kind of kindness. Any kindness at all will do. The significance of a cup of cold water will be hard to grasp for those who have never been thirsty. If we are in an air-conditioned building full of water fountains and water coolers, a cold cup of water will mean very little. Certainly appreciated. But forgettable. It will seem ordinary, mundane even. The same for smiles.

Deep down, we do not really think this kind of kindness is important. As far as we are concerned, it will get no press before God or men. Heck, I feel weird writing about it.

It's the big stuff which looks excellent on spiritual resumés, and it's these we use to determine the authenticity of the faith of God's people. The smaller acts of kindness? They not only do not show up, but their absence is justified by the former.

"I know he is a jackass, and hard on the wait staff at restaurants, but he gives a lot to missions!"

"Oh, well then."

Neither should negate the other. Neither the small acts of everyday nor the noteworthy should make the other obsolete. Both are needed, sure. But one is mundane and therefore forgone. And forgotten. We forget the need. We forget the power. And we forget the words of Christ, who would commend the mundane kindness of a cup of cold water.

I imagine that most of us cannot see the significant moments of kindness because our lives are so full of the like. The meaning gets lost in the volume. So we naturally see kindness in the newsworthy acts of philanthropy we either want to receive or be noted for.

After all, no one notices the smile — it disappears in a wisp. Poof! It is gone. The cold water is no sooner enjoyed than forgotten in the desire for another. So we forgo these kinds of things altogether. They lack significance in a world we are always being told we can change. Kindness has no cataclysmic effect on the forces of evil in the name of justice. So we leave it off on our way to end injustice.

In other words, we want to end war, hunger and poverty

in our lifetime. But we do not posses the will to let someone merge in front of us in traffic, and do so with a smile.

In "a dry and weary land" a cup of cold water is the picture of kindness. Though small, the refreshment is needed, appreciated and not easily forgotten by the one who needs it most.

This is hard because we are prone to define kindness by the largest possible measure. The plumb line for what is kind is far removed from the stuff of smiles and cups of cold water. It exists in the form of checks and gifts, voluminous and weighty. And all the while, as we plan on newsworthy acts of good works, there are moments of opportunity.

Perhaps only a smile is possible. A holding of the door. An offer of assistance. That cup of cold water. All mundane, but every single one an opportunity for kindness to break in on a life just as the rays of the sun break in on a morning.

CHAPTER FOURTEEN

The Room Must Grow

The port, well worth the cruise, is near,
And every wave is charmed

Ralph Waldo Emerson, "Terminus"

There is a vague memory of my grandparents' house I can claim: a huge A-frame home with a great big great room, complete with stairs climbing, and climbing, and climbing. In this memory, the Winnie-the-Pooh footie pajamas are worn with pride. I'm coming down the stairs. There is a magnificent Christmas tree reaching into the towering cathedral of a roof. The room is wide-eyed, mouth-opened massive. Lots of dark wood on all sides.

Driving by that house a few dozen times as an adult revealed the honest-to-God truth: the place is not quite as big as I remember. In fact, it seems small in comparison. I'm still disappointed, and work up scenarios that alter the reality. My physical growth and a little bit of perspective have changed the way I view such spaces. It is a disappointing thing for this to happen, for I would prefer to have kept the memory intact along with the wonder.

After we moved into the house we now live in, every day for a month or more my son would inevitably say, "this is the greatest and biggest house ever!" And he wasn't just excited. He was convicted on the matter. And he would proclaim it sometimes like he needed to convert us to his way of thinking.

After a month of living in this house, it dawned on me one summer-scorched morning why he might be so adamant about this. It probably had a lot in common with my memory of my mom's parents' home. My son is only four years old, and the kitchen/living/dining area with the drama of an arched ceiling held in place by exposed wood beams must seem huge to his vertically-challenged frame. It feels like a big, wide-open space to me. I can only imagine how enormous he must think it is.

But he will grow up and look at pictures of this room and wonder how he could think it was so magically big. When driving by with wife and kids, he will declare to them how big the house was for him. He will be disappointed, as we all are about these things. And this phenomenon is not relegated to only homes either. Parks, hills, automobiles, churches and people themselves shrink as we grow up and older. This is the way of things.

But not everything.

As I have grown, some things have grown larger and become far more significant than I could have ever believed possible. As a young man with boyhood stretched over me still, I thought I was beginning to really understand the world. Older now, I know less than I did then.

The exact opposite of what happened with my memory of my grandparents' home is happening with my understanding of God and what it means to live by faith. The room is growing larger, not smaller. And with the growth of the room, the magic of it all extends out into places unseen before.

As a young man, I imagined the Christian life — separate from the rest of life — as one of 1) accepting Jesus as my Savior, 2) being good, 3) telling others about Jesus. This was pretty much it. A small room indeed. A comfortable room. But as I grew up, the room grew also. God started having to do with more parts of my life than just my morality, and who I had witnessed to recently, and where I would spend eternity. Just now I'm realizing, after many years of this, how reality has been working on me.

It shocks me a little. For I'm cynical enough to think the familiarity of The Story would make it all the more constricting. Doesn't familiarity breed contempt?

But instead, everything is enlarging. God now has to do with everything. Everything. And not just my own little need to escape hell.

The room has become a universe of inexhaustible ideas,

and feelings, and compulsions, and passions, and dreams, and hopes. No longer am I inhabiting the closet-like space of getting people to walk an aisle, and fill out a card, and be good while doing so, and then supposing we have lived the Christian life. The claustrophobia of such a space would kill me now.

Not now. I've now sat in the room of hovering stars being called by name, and an earth groaning under the weight of original sin. The room of the impoverished the world over, and chefs who can work culinary miracles with the raw materials of creation. The room of disabilities and exceptional abilities. The room of weariness and wonder. The room of sexuality and suffering. The room of grace, and mercy, and failure, and falling. A room so big, idealism is lost.

The gospel story does this. Or should. The room grew inexplicably large for the Jews who followed Jesus very soon after his death. It grew from a religion of Jews to one of the whole world. One sin we just might be in danger of committing but rarely (if ever) discuss is the transgression of limiting the Christian life to just a few things we can check off. All good things to be sure. Feed the poor. No adultery. Be nice. You know, the usual suspects. But this is all our imaginations can, well, imagine. It's just so small and easy to deal with.

But what I cannot help but feel — no, hope for — is the believing life to be oh so much bigger and grander than this. I want to believe my faith in the gospel of grace is not limited to the "spiritual" things but is exploding onto every single mundane moment in my life. I want the shrapnel of this explosion to embed itself in every enjoyment, and failure, and celebration, and tragedy coming my way.

We have fallen into thinking that simply because the Christian faith is not less than what it was when we first began, then it needs be no more. Certainly the Christian life is not less than believe, do good and tell. But just because it is not smaller than this room does not mean it should not be bigger. Experience and the scriptures[1] themselves go nuclear against such an idea.

The room must grow.

Sometimes I look into the details of the story of all God

1 See I Corinthians 10:31, John 2:1-12, and Romans 8:28 (ESV).

has done and a world opens up, dwarfing the one I lived, and moved, and breathed in moments earlier. And other times I look into the crevices of my own life and as I am clearing away the oil and dirt, the grime and contaminants, the room expands.

But we cannot make the room grow. There is no formula. Just as we cannot make ourselves grow in age, we do not necessarily wake up one day in a room that has grown. It is the non-work of patience over many seasons of seeing God and what he has done, with wonder.

This is why I like growing older. I've no desire to be young again. This would be like trading the great outdoors of a faith for the space of pantries. This growing faith that takes in the world bit by bit, and takes on years and decades, is another pushing back of the Fall. The Fall requires our lives, and coldly demands we trade in beating hearts for silent ones. But this Fall takes a body blow when we prefer the aging body with the growing faith. For the room to grow we must also be willing to exchange bodies of nubility and virility for minds fit for Kingdom expansion.

There is nothing more ordinary than aging. The ravages of time are a great equalizer. This is level ground. No one has a leg up on anyone else. Money cannot stay time's march. It goose-steps and leaves crow's feet around every single eye. Sure, we can fake it with lasers and injections. But calendars are not known to lie. They are relentlessly found to be true. And the more we are unwilling to release the hands of the clock, the more ridiculous we become.

A great reversal is taking place within us. We grow up and age and must deal with sagging buttocks and breasts. Hair silvers and then falls. Backs bend and joints ache. However, a larger reality is overtaking even this. Even though we must age for us to grow in our faith, the growth is taking us back to the wonder of small bodies in cavernous spaces. This must be the child-like faith Jesus spoke of. My hope is to sit one day with aching bones, skin no longer taut, and senses failing and say, "this is the greatest house ever."

CHAPTER FIFTEEN

Be Nobody Special

Everybody wants you to be special.

Ryan Adams, "Rescue Blues"

Some people read books carefully, like the rich sip tea. Me? I'm like a biker in a sports bar without a napkin. I tear through books like a hungry college student on wing night. Because of this, I miss things. My comprehension is weird. I can recall passages and see them on the actual page like I just sat the book down. But very often, I'll be reading a book for the third time and see something — a scene, for instance — and it is wholly new to me. Virgin literary territory untouched by my eyes. It's because I read so fast. Just not well.

Earlier this year I read book five of The Chronicles of Narnia, *The Horse and His Boy*. I have been reading these books for years, since I was a young boy. My mind swims in the scenes of Narnia. But I don't read them for intellectual stimulation. I'm still that young boy.

Does it happen to everyone who rereads books over and over? I'm doing the revved-up reading version of left-hand turns at Talladega, and a scene makes me sit up and take notice. I actually look at the cover to see if this is the version I am most familiar with — like they would have added this chapter later (or something equally nefarious), when no one was looking.

There is a scene that includes a short speech by the Hermit of the Southern March. He is talking to Bree, the talking horse, who is on his way home to Narnia after being in slavery along with so many non-talking horses, thank you very much:

"My good Horse," said the Hermit..."my good Horse, you've lost nothing but your self-conceit. No, no, cousin. Don't put back your ears and shake your mane at me. If you are really so humbled as you sounded a minute ago, you must learn to listen to sense. You're not quite the great Horse you had come to think, from living among poor dumb horses. Of course you were braver and cleverer than them. You could hardly help being that. It doesn't follow that you'll be anyone very special in Narnia. But as long as you know you're nobody special, you'll be a very decent sort of Horse, on the whole, and taking one thing with another."

Here is a message never once heard out in the real world. From the pages of a children's book read by millions, but repeated by no one, a call rings out into a sky where everyone is to be the star and no one is to be the blackness behind it.

This is the message you will never hear in schools, TV commercials, or churches. In fact you will hear the very opposite.

"You are special!" is the mantra.

The idea is everyone is really, really special. And to a point, I suppose it is true. We all have different hues of character. All are marked by varied memories peculiar to our lives. Physical and emotional buoys signal deep waters of places only we have explored. And so we buy in.

But if everyone is special then no one is special. So, then, of course, the goal is to be more special by doing special, specialized things. Distinguishing ourselves.

Schools tell us, "you are innately special, so do something special and change the world."

The commercials declare, "you are special, buy our product, change the world."

And the evangelical churches?

There are two kinds of pastors in the main: those who speak at conferences with green rooms (you think I'm kidding? They have green rooms. With spring water, I guess), and those who want to do so. The men who lead our churches into faithfulness have little gremlins tugging at their ego, telling them they are not doing anything special unless they are being distinguished.

How could they possibly have any other message besides one in which the listener walks away with the purpose of doing something special to change the world? All for the glory of God.

I mean, who would want to be a person no one has ever heard of? What kind of person just goes about their business in this rock star culture? What pastor or pew-sitter wants to remain nameless, in year-in and year-out obscurity? When fame and reputation and notoriety are ripe for the picking? Why would we be Greta Garbo, dodging the public, when there's YouTube?

But I say, be nobody special. Do your job. Take care of your family. Clean your house. Mow your yard. Read your Bible. Attend worship. Pray. Watch your life and doctrine closely. Love your spouse. Love your kids. Be generous. Laugh with your friends. Drink your wine heartily. Eat your meat lustily. Be honest. Be kind to your waitress. Expect no special treatment. And do it all quietly.

You want to be a spiritual hero? Distinguish yourself? Ironically, you have to give it up. This sounds like, "lose your life so you can save it"[1] for a reason. Being nobody special will feel like losing your life, maybe the life you've dreamed of in front of the mirror. In front of the pastor, or as a pastor. But to distinguish yourself in our world, you must be happy about being a nobody.

This little book is not a call to do nothing. It is a call to be faithful right where you are, regardless of how mundane that place is.

The need is to go full bore, with wild willingness, into a life full of the mundane, armed to the teeth with the belief we are featured in the Story God will forever be telling with joy. We are all just bit players, sure. But that is why we should be fine with being nobody special in the story being told. I know God is not the long-bearded grandfather up in the sky, the one we pictured while sitting in midget-sized chairs before Sunday school felt boards. But we liked the picture in our head for a reason. There is something about the kindness of sitting on the knee of our Father, and Him smiling while we talk of nothing particularly extraordinary about ourselves. And Him caring

---

1   See Matthew 10:39 (ESV).

still.

The zeitgeist of this age is we should let nothing stop us from being special. And especially vulnerable to these sermons are the young people, who after a semester of college are now experts at being special.

Sacred and secular alike, the proclaimers of this message are nothing if not earnest. And it is not hard to imagine why. Telling someone they are not special sounds cruel. I understand.

But I disagree.

The "you're nobody special" message may be the most freeing message of all. Especially for those who have the banner of "mundane" flying kite-high over their life. Now you can just be yourself. Over against being the abstract, "special," you can land on the hard concrete reality of being yourself. Only more so. No need to be the pie-in-the-sky version of someone else's idea of what special is. You can now just love God, love others and be nobody. And as long as you know this — "...you're nobody special — you'll be a very decent sort of horse, on the whole, and taking one thing with another."

Acknowledgements

Without the support, encouragement, and love of my wife, Bethany, this book would never have been written. In so many ways, this book is for her.

This book started taking shape a few months into a year of immersing myself in the writings of Eugene Peterson. He unwittingly mentored me through much of these writings. I will forever be thankful.

Thanks to all of my family but special thanks to my parents who always bought me books. Book-lovers themselves, my mom will read this whole book to my dad. And that will make it all worth it.

This book was written in the context of a circle of friends. They deserve more thanks than I can give — the Damerons, Edwards, all the Heads, the Mackles, the Gleasons, the Blaisings, the Tappans, and many more.

In 5th grade, after I talked bad about poetry, Mrs. Derieux dragged me out in the hall and gave me a good talking to, a book by Shel Silverstein, and a lifelong love of words.

If there's a soundtrack to this little book, it's Springsteen's "Darkness On the Edge of Town." An album about the harsh realities of adult life, I listed to it over and over while writing and editing these essays.

Thanks to my friends at Kalos Press for the chance.

Thanks to God for all the echoes and stars.

About
Matthew B. Redmond

Matt Redmond was born in Birmingham, AL. He attended Southeastern Bible College and Covenant Theological Seminary, and has served in pastoral ministry in four different congregations. Matt currently works in the banking industry.

Matt and his wife Bethany have three children: Emma, Knox, and Dylan. Matt's writing has been published by the Gospel Coalition and other publications. He also writes a blog: Echoes and Stars.

Matt began writing *The God Of The Mundane* because he realized that contemporary portrayals of the God of the Bible left little room for a God who was concerned about ordinary things. Building on his conviction that the biblical God was an everyday God, Matt's reflections on this topic coalesced into a nascent collection of essays.

About
Kalos Press

Kalos Press was established to give a voice to literary fiction, memoir, devotional writing, and Christian Reflection, of excellent quality, outside of the mainstream Christian publishing industry.

We believe that good writing is beautiful in form and in function, and is capable of being an instrument of transformation. It is our hope and ambition that every title produced by Kalos Press will live up to this belief.

For more information about Kalos Press, *The Exact Place*, and/or our other titles, or for ordering information, visit us on our website: www.kalospress.org, or contact us by e-mail at info@kalospress.org.

Digital Copies Of
The God Of The Mundane

At Kalos Press, we've found that we often appreciate owning both print and digital editions of the books we read; perhaps you have found this as well. In our gratitude to you for purchasing a print version of this book, we are pleased to offer you free copies of the digital editions of *The God Of The Mundane*. To obtain one or more of these, follow the link embedded in the Quick Response (QR) Code below. Thank you for your support!